Terrifying to Touch!

DEADLY ANIMALS

by Alex Hall

Minneapolis, Minnesota

Credits
Cover and title page, © Dirk Ercken/Shutterstock; 4TL, © Joseph B. O'Connell /Adobe Stock; 4B, © Tomas Drahos/Shutterstock; 5TL, CORREIA Patrice/Adobe Stock; 5R, © Howard Chen/iStock; 6, © Rawisyah Aditya/Shutterstock; 7, M.E.Reid/ Adobe Stock; 8, © Conservationist/Shutterstock; 9, © e.borneoland/Shutterstock; 10, © Thor-sten Spoerlein/Shutterstock; 11, © kikkerdirk/iStock; 12, © Juan Sangiovan-ni/ Shutterstock; 13, © Ondrej Prosicky/iStock 14, feathercollector/Shutterstock; 15, © Benjamin Freeman/Wikimedia Commons; 16, © Martin Pelanek/Shutterstock; 17, © Ash - stock.adobe.com/Adobe Stock; 18, © Danny Ye/Shutterstock; 19, © DANNY YE/ Adobe Stock; 20, © Thierry Ei-denweil/Shutterstock; 21, © YUSRAN ABDUL RAHMAN/ Shutterstock; 22, © Vitalii Hu-lai/Shutterstock; 23,© as3d/iStock; 24, © Johan Holmdahl/ iStock; 25, © Nicoproductions/iStock; 26, © teekayu/Shutterstock; 27, © Mariia /Adobe Stock; 28, © Thorsten Spoer-lein/Shutterstock; 29, © Thorsten Spoerlein/Adobe Stock; 30TL, © Freder/iStock; 30B, © asbtkb /Adobe Stock

Bearport Publishing Company Product Development Team
Publisher: Jen Jenson; Director of Product Development: Spencer Brinker; Editorial Director: Allison Juda; Editor: Cole Nelson; Editor: Tiana Tran; Production Editor: Naomi Reich; Art Director: Kim Jones; Designer: Kayla Eggert; Designer: Steve Scheluchin; Production Specialist: Owen Hamlin

Library of Congress Cataloging-in-Publication Data is available at www.loc.gov or upon request from the publisher.

ISBN: 979-8-89577-090-0 (hardcover)
ISBN: 979-8-89577-533-2 (paperback)
ISBN: 979-8-89577-207-2 (ebook)

© 2026 BookLife Publishing
This edition is published by arrangement with BookLife Publishing.

North American adaptations © 2026 Bearport Publishing Company. All rights reserved. No part of this publication may be reproduced in whole or in part, stored in any retrieval system, or transmitted in any form or by any means, electronic, mechanical, photocopying, recording, or otherwise, without written permission from the publisher. Bearport Publishing is a division of FlutterBee Education Group.

For more information, write to Bearport Publishing, 3500 American Blvd W, Suite 150, Bloomington, MN 55431.

Contents

A World of Killer Critters 4
Stay Back! 6
Slow Loris 8
Golden Poison Frog 10
Cane Toad 12
Hooded Pitohui 14
Platypus 16
Electric Eel 18
Blue-Ringed Octopus 20
Freshwater Snail 22
Pufferfish 24
Porcupine 26
The Deadliest to Touch! 28
Critters Everywhere 30
Glossary 31
Index 32
Read More 32
Learn More Online 32

A World of Killer Critters

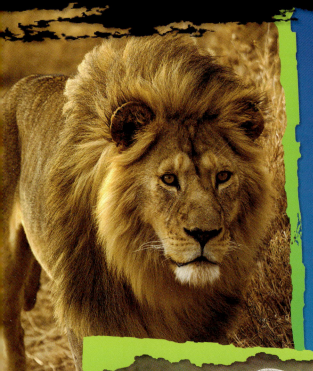

The world is full of wonderful, wild, and dangerous critters! Animals everywhere have lots of different ways to defend themselves. This should make you think twice before coming close.

Whether an animal looks cozy or killer, it's best to watch out! It might just spike, bite, prick, or shock you when you least expect it.

READ ON TO LEARN MORE ABOUT SOME OF THE WORLD'S SCARIEST ANIMALS TO TOUCH . . . IF YOU DARE!

Stay Back!

Beware! One of the ways animals stay safe is to carry killer venom or cover their skin with deadly **toxin**. But what makes these animals so terrifying to touch?

When some animals are touched, their powerful venoms and toxins tear apart bodies from the inside. Now that's painful!

Touching animals can be dangerous in other ways, too. Some animals have spiky skin, while others produce electric shocks. But it's the ones with deadly toxins that you really have to look out for.

Let's take a look at some killer critters and score how dangerous they are. We'll rate their bite damage, their toxic effects, and how harmful they are to touch. Which animal will win this deadly competition?

Slow Loris

Who is the first competitor? It's the slow loris! While this big-eyed **primate** may seem harmless, it has a killer secret up its furry sleeves.

The slow loris has venomous **glands** near its elbows. When the creature licks its glands, the venom mixes with the saliva on its tongue. This prepares the primate to deliver a toxic bite. *CHOMP!*

One bite and the slow loris's deadly venom can cause a burning feeling in the throat. Then, the venom attacks the heart and lungs.

KILLER CRITTER SCORECARD

BITE DANGER	5	
HARMFUL TO TOUCH	1	
VENOM DANGER	5	
BODY DAMAGE	3	

SLOW LORIS

TOTAL 14

Golden Poison Frog

Many types of poison dart frogs have brightly colored skin. This serves as a warning to would-be **predators**. The frog is toxic! The deadliest of all poison frogs is the golden poison frog.

This **amphibian** lives in the wet and warm tropical rainforests of South America. It uses its powerful back legs to jump and get around.

Within minutes, a single drop of its toxin can **paralyze** its victim. The unlucky person has only 10 minutes before it's lights out. And just one golden poison frog has enough toxin to kill as many as 10 people.

KILLER CRITTER SCORECARD

GOLDEN POISON FROG

BITE DANGER	4
HARMFUL TO TOUCH	10
TOXIN DANGER	10
BODY DAMAGE	8

TOTAL 32

Cane Toad

Let's check out this dry, warty amphibian. The cane toad originally comes from South and Central America. It has rapidly crept into new territories, including Australia and the United States.

Cane toads were first introduced to Australia as a method of pest control. However, soon their numbers multiplied. Today, they are an **invasive** species in the country.

If a cane toad senses danger, it releases dangerous poison from glands behind its shoulders. The poison can cause paralysis, heart problems, and even death in animals that touch it. It is only deadly to humans if the toxin gets inside their bodies.

KILLER CRITTER SCORECARD

CANE TOAD

BITE DANGER	2
HARMFUL TO TOUCH	5
TOXIN DANGER	7
BODY DAMAGE	3

TOTAL 17

Hooded Pitohui

This bird's bright orange color is the only sign that predators need to stay away. The hooded pitohui is one of the few known poisonous birds.

What makes the hooded pitohui so deadly? The bird feeds on poisonous beetles, making its skin and feathers highly toxic. One touch of the toxin can make animals go numb.

For humans, touching the hooded pitohui's feathers causes a burning feeling on the skin. But if the toxin somehow gets in the body, it can have deadly consequences.

KILLER CRITTER SCORECARD

HOODED PITOHUI

BITE DANGER	4	
HARMFUL TO TOUCH	3	
TOXIN DANGER	4	
BODY DAMAGE	5	

TOTAL: 16

Platypus

Platypuses can be found swimming in the waters of Australia. Although these furry **mammals** may seem harmless, they have a deadly secret.

Male platypuses have spikes called spurs on the back of their ankles. These spurs are connected to a venom gland. This venom allows the animals to defend themselves against predators.

For small animals, platypus venom can be deadly. Luckily for humans, it is not strong enough to kill. At most, people feel intense pain caused by the cut from a spur.

KILLER CRITTER SCORECARD

BITE DANGER	1	
HARMFUL TO TOUCH	2	
VENOM DANGER	3	
BODY DAMAGE	7	

PLATYPUS

TOTAL: 13

Electric Eel

Despite their name, electric eels aren't actually eels. They are knifefish that are found swimming in the waters of South America.

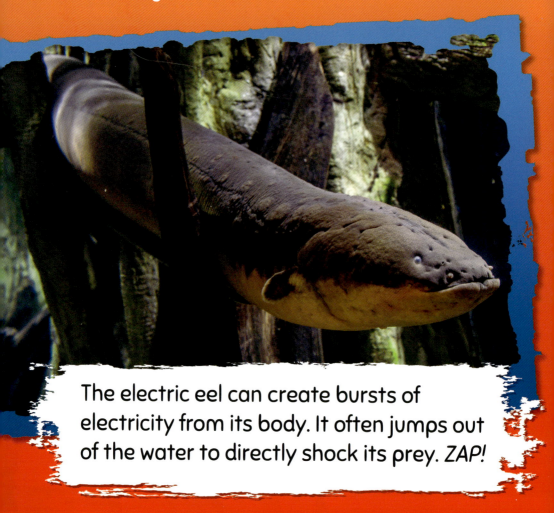

The electric eel can create bursts of electricity from its body. It often jumps out of the water to directly shock its prey. ZAP!

Getting shocked by these snakelike creatures can hurt. It may cause heart problems and trigger trouble breathing. Sometimes, this can lead to death!

KILLER CRITTER SCORECARD

ELECTRIC EEL

BITE DANGER	1	
HARMFUL TO TOUCH	0	
VENOM DANGER	0	
BODY DAMAGE	6	

TOTAL **7**

Blue-Ringed Octopus

The blue-ringed octopus is named for the blue circles on its body. However, these bright spots only appear as a warning. The octopus may be ready to attack with its venomous bite.

This octopus lives in the warm waters of the Indian and Pacific Oceans, where it dines on crabs and shrimp. With its strong suckers, catching prey is an easy task for the octopus.

Sometimes, people get too close to blue-ringed octopuses. If this happens, the eight-armed creatures respond with a venomous bite. Once the venom gets into a person's blood, they could die within 20 minutes!

KILLER CRITTER SCORECARD

BITE DANGER	8	
HARMFUL TO TOUCH	6	
VENOM DANGER	10	
BODY DAMAGE	7	

BLUE-RINGED OCTOPUS

TOTAL: 31

Freshwater Snail

Want to go swimming? Many different species of freshwater snails make their homes in lakes, rivers, and ponds. However, they make the waters from South America to Asia dangerous.

Unlike most critter competitors, freshwater snails can kill from a distance. These creatures turn water into pools of death!

Many **parasites** live on the freshwater snail. The parasites spread through water when the critter takes a dip. Parasites can carry diseases that stop the body from working properly. A single splash in some dirty water could be deadly.

KILLER CRITTER SCORECARD

FRESHWATER SNAIL

BITE DANGER	0
HARMFUL TO TOUCH	0
DISEASE DANGER	7
BODY DAMAGE	3

TOTAL: 10

Pufferfish

Don't play with this inflatable ball! Pufferfish get their name from how they puff up their bodies with water. When this happens, the spines on their skin stick out.

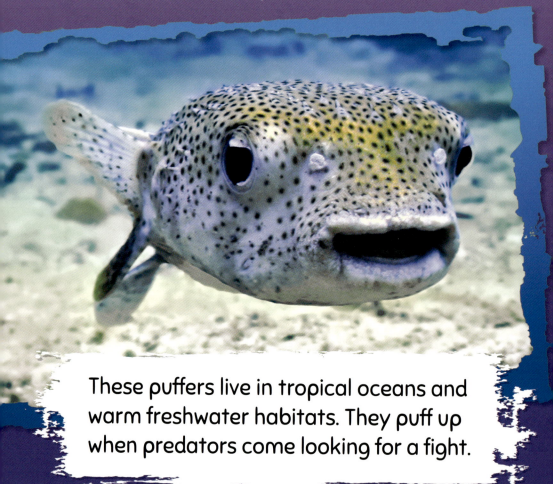

These puffers live in tropical oceans and warm freshwater habitats. They puff up when predators come looking for a fight.

Pufferfish are not just dangerous because they are spiky. Their bodies are also very toxic. Some pufferfish have toxins strong enough to kill creatures that eat them.

KILLER CRITTER SCORECARD

PUFFERFISH

BITE DANGER	0	
HARMFUL TO TOUCH	8	
TOXIN DANGER	5	
BODY DAMAGE	4	

TOTAL: 17

Porcupine

When you think of a dangerous animal to touch, a porcupine may come to mind. This prickly critter has about 30,000 quills on its body. It uses these sharp spikes to defend itself. Stay back!

When predators get too close, porcupines make their quills stand up. Quills fall off easily when touched. Over time, porcupines slowly grow new quills to replace their old ones.

Animals often die from porcupine quills. The barbed tips from quills attach themselves to predators, making them hard to remove. Although humans will live through the jabs, the quills are still extremely painful and dangerous.

KILLER CRITTER SCORECARD

PORCUPINE

BITE DANGER	0	
HARMFUL TO TOUCH	0	
VENOM DANGER	0	
BODY DAMAGE	7	

TOTAL: 7

The Deadliest to Touch!

Who comes out on top in this killer critter competition? The golden poison frog wins!

While this frog isn't the biggest animal in the competition, its fast reflexes and toxic skin make it the deadly winner.

A person who touches a golden poison frog would soon feel numb. Before long, the toxin may paralyze their body. And within minutes, the victim could be dead!

Unluckily for us, scientists have yet to find a cure. The best way to stay safe is to not touch the golden poison frog in the first place!

Critters Everywhere

The world is a big place, full of amazing animals. But the next time you see a wild critter, do not touch. It might have toxic skin, a venomous bite, or a spiky body!

Glossary

amphibian an animal that can live both on land and in water

glands types of organs in the body that produce chemicals

invasive a plant or animal that is not from a place and spreads in a harmful way

male an animal that cannot give birth to young

mammals animals that have warm blood, a backbone, and produce milk

paralyze to lose feeling in or the ability to move a body part

parasites living things that feed off others to survive

predators animals that hunt and eat other animals

primate the group of animals that contains humans, apes, and monkeys

toxin a harmful substance produced by a plant or animal

Index

blood 21
electricity 18
feathers 14–15
glands 8, 13
oceans 24
parasites 23
quills 26–27
saliva 8, 21
spines 24
spurs 16–17
toxins 6, 11, 14–15, 25, 29

Read More

Bolte, Mari. *Sharp and Spiky Animal Weapons and Defenses (Shockingly Strange Animal Weapons and Defenses).* North Mankato, MN: Capstone Press, 2024.

Grodzicki, Jenna. *Poison Dart Frog (Library of Awesome Animals).* Minneapolis: Bearport Publishing Company, 2023.

Temple, Colton. *Amazing Animal Electricity (Animal Superpowers!).* Minneapolis: Kaleidoscope, 2021.

Learn More Online

1. Go to **FactSurfer.com** or scan the QR code below.
2. Enter "**Terrifying Touch**" into the search box.
3. Click on the cover of this book to see a list of websites.